OMAN TRAVEL GUIDE

A Comprehensive Traveler's Handbook To Help you embark On An Enchanting Journey To unveil The Secrets Of Arabian Wonders

Michele Allison

COPYRIGHT

Every aspect of this publication is protected, and reproduction, distribution, or transmission in any manner, such as photocopying, recording, or other electronic or mechanical methods, is strictly prohibited without the publisher's prior written consent. However, limited exceptions are made for brief quotations incorporated into critical reviews and specific noncommercial uses permitted by copyright law.

Copyright © Michele Allison 2024

TABLE OF CONTENT

CHAPTER ONE — 6
Introduction to Oman — 6
   Overview of Oman — 6
   Geography and Climate — 9
   Culture and History — 12
   Language and Communications — 16

CHAPTER TWO — 20
Travel Planning — 20
   Best Time to Visit — 20
   Budgeting Tips — 23
   Visa Requirements — 27
   Itinerary Planning — 33
   Safety and Health — 37

CHAPTER THREE — 42
Transportation — 42
   Air Travel — 42
   Public / Local Transport Options — 45

CHAPTER FOUR — 49
Accommodations — 49
   Hotel Options and Budget Lodging — 49
   Resorts — 52

CHAPTER FIVE — 56
Dining and Cuisine — 56
- Popular Restaurant and Local Dishes — 56
- Eating Etiquette — 60

CHAPTER SIX — 64
Attractions and Activities — 64
- Must-See Sites — 64
- Adventure Activities — 69
- Shopping Destinations — 71

CHAPTER SEVEN — 75
Family Travel — 75
- Family-Friendly Attractions — 75

CHAPTER EIGHT — 82
Business Travel — 82
- Business Etiquette — 82
- Meeting Facilities — 87

CHAPTER NINE — 93
Resources — 93
- Emergency Contacts — 93
- Useful Apps — 96
- Travel Insurance — 100
- Common Phrases — 104
- Language Etiquette — 113

Conclusion and Additional Tips — 116

Safety Tips	116
Sustainable Travel Tips	119
Final Recommendations	122

CHAPTER ONE

Introduction to Oman

Overview of Oman

Oman, a country with a seamless fusion of modernity and tradition, is tucked away on the southeast tip of the Arabian Peninsula. This multicultural nation with a wealth of natural beauty, history, and culture is located where the mountains and sea meet.

Oman's diversity is ingrained in its fundamental fiber. As soon as you set foot in its captivating surroundings, you'll be encircled by an astounding variety of scenery, including untamed beaches, verdant oases, and rough mountains and deserts. The Sultanate's terrain is breathtakingly beautiful and diverse.

From the moment of arrival, one feels the warmth of Omani hospitality. The genuine experiences that locals relate are priceless treasures here. The inhabitants of the country greet guests warmly because of their rich history and customs. Travelers are welcomed with authentic warmth and hospitality, whether they are participating in a lively market negotiation or having a leisurely talk over Omani coffee.

Oman has a long and distinguished past. Through a journey characterized by tenacity, power, and vision, the Sultanate has transitioned from the once-mighty maritime empire of the eighth century to the contemporary Renaissance of the twentieth century. The country's historic castles, forts, and archaeological monuments attest to its rich history and position as a key historical crossroads.

Oman's cultural landscape is as diverse and rich as its physical terrain. The nation's traditional arts, music, and dance are highly valued and provide tourists with a window into its essence. Omani food is a culinary experience to be cherished, with its exquisite fusion of flavors and spices. Every dish has a narrative, from the fragrant kahwa to the luscious shuwa.

Oman is a land of exploration and adventure, even beyond its wealth in history and culture. There are plenty of things to do for those who enjoy the great outdoors, from diving in clear waters brimming with marine life to walking through untamed mountain scenery. The country's immaculate natural reserves and protected areas are testaments to its dedication to ecotourism and sustainable development.

The shores of Oman entice those looking for peace and quiet. The Sultanate is endowed with many miles of scenic beaches and quiet harbors along its pristine coastline. The country has an abundance of experiences to fulfill the needs of any traveler, from the peaceful beaches of Salalah to the busy streets of Muscat.

Oman's dedication to innovation and growth is demonstrated by the country's ascent to prominence as a modern, progressive nation.

With its contemporary highways, airports, and transit networks, the Sultanate's infrastructure facilitates easy and effective domestic travel. After a long day of exploring, the country's top-notch hotels and resorts offer elegance and coziness, making them the ideal getaway.

Oman offers countless experiences and opportunities. The Sultanate has much to offer every type of visitor, from its stunning natural surroundings and rich cultural legacy to its contemporary conveniences and modern history. Oman promises to enthrall and inspire those seeking adventure, leisure, or cultural immersion.

Geography and Climate

Geographically, Oman is separated into several regions, each with its own particular characteristics. The coastal areas of Muscat, Sohar, and Salalah are distinguished by their beautiful beaches, lush oases, and bustling fishing settlements. Inland, the scenery changes to rocky mountains and immense desert stretches like the Wahiba Sands and Rub' al Khali, where towering dunes reach as far as the eye can see.

The northern coast of Oman has a Mediterranean climate, with colder temperatures and more rainfall than the rest of the nation. This region is home to Oman's highest mountain range, the Al Hajar Mountains, which provide breathtaking vistas and outdoor activities including trekking and rock climbing. The mountainous region also includes Jebel Shams, widely known as the "Grand Canyon of Arabia," which has stunning cliffs and deep canyons.

Central Oman's geography is dominated by desert plains and rolling hills. The historic town of Nizwa, with its traditional souks and majestic fortress, is nearby, as is Adam, an old city noted for its prehistoric tombs and petroglyphs.

Southern Oman, including Salalah, has a tropical climate with lush flora and ample rainfall. This region is recognized for its gorgeous beaches, especially the stunning Al Mughsail Beach, as well as its rich cultural legacy, which includes historic monuments like the UNESCO-listed Al Baleed Archaeological Park.

The climate in Oman varies according to the time of year and location. Summers can be extremely hot, with temperatures exceeding 45°C (113°F) in some regions, although winters are cooler, with temperatures ranging from 15°C to 25°C (59°F to 77°F). Rainfall is scarce in most regions of the country, with the exception of the southern region around Salalah, which has a monsoon season from June to September.

Oman's diverse landscapes and temperatures make it a popular destination for a wide range of travelers. Oman has something for everyone, whether you want to go on an adventure in the desert, relax on the beach, or learn about local culture in historic villages. And, with its contemporary infrastructure and inviting hospitality, exploring this beautiful country will be an unforgettable experience.

Culture and History

The Sultanate of Oman is a country rich in history and culture, with a heritage that dates back thousands of years. Located on the southeastern coast of the Arabian Peninsula, Oman has been shaped by a variety of influences, including its strategic location along ancient trade routes and its long history of maritime trade.

Religion plays a significant role in Omani culture, with the majority of the population adhering to Islam. Islam is not only a religious belief but also a way of life, guiding the daily activities and interactions of Omani people. The religious practices observed in Oman are in accordance with the Sunni branch of Islam and follow the Maliki school of Islamic jurisprudence.

Muslims in Oman observe the five daily prayers prescribed by Islam. These prayers are Fajr (pre-dawn), Dhuhr (noon), Asr (afternoon), Maghrib (just after sunset), and Isha (evening). The times of these prayers are determined by the position of the sun and change throughout the year. The call to prayer, known as the Adhan, is called from mosques across the country, inviting Muslims to stop what they are doing and join in the prayer.

Ramadan is the ninth month of the Islamic lunar calendar and is considered the holiest month in Islam. During Ramadan, Muslims in Oman fast from dawn until sunset, abstaining from food, drink, smoking, and other physical needs. The fast is broken each evening with a meal called Iftar, which is often a communal gathering shared with family and friends. Ramadan is also a time for increased religious devotion, with Muslims spending more time in prayer, reading the Quran, and engaging in acts of charity. The end of Ramadan is marked by the celebration of

Eid al-Fitr, a joyous holiday that includes communal prayers, feasting, and giving of gifts.

Eid Al-Adha Also known as the Festival of Sacrifice, Eid al-Adha commemorates the willingness of Prophet Ibrahim (Abraham) to sacrifice his son as an act of obedience to God. Muslims in Oman mark this occasion with special prayers, acts of charity, and the sacrifice of an animal, typically a sheep or goat. The meat from the sacrificed animal is then distributed among family, friends, and those in need.

Friday is considered a special day for Muslims, and they gather at mosques for the Jumu'ah prayers. This weekly gathering is an opportunity for communal worship and the listening to a sermon (khutbah) delivered by the imam (religious leader). The Jumu'ah prayers are considered obligatory for men, while women have the option to attend if they wish.

Visiting the Holy Mosque in Mecca (Hajj), the Hajj is a pilgrimage to the holy city of Mecca in

Saudi Arabia, which is one of the Five Pillars of Islam. Muslims who are physically and financially able are required to perform the Hajj at least once in their lifetime. The Hajj takes place in the Islamic month of Dhu al-Hijjah and involves several days of rituals and prayers.

Omanis are noted for their generosity and warmth, welcome guests and sharing their culture and traditions. Traditional Omani apparel, including the dishdasha for men and the abaya for women, is still widely worn, and traditional traditions such as falaj (a network of water canals) and barasti (palm-fronddwellings) are also part of daily life in rural areas.

In the modern era, Oman has experienced remarkable expansion and progress, thanks to visionary leadership that has prioritized education, infrastructure, and economic diversification. The country's dedication to progress is reflected in its world-class infrastructure, which includes modern airports, highways, and ports, as well as investments in renewable energy, healthcare, and education.

Despite its modernity, Oman maintains a strong sense of national identity and pride in its history. The Sultanate's dedication to preserving its culture and history is demonstrated by its efforts to safeguard and promote archeological sites, forts, and cultural landmarks, ensuring that future generations can experience and appreciate Oman's rich cultural heritage.

Language and Communications

Language is a vital and important component of Omani culture, and being familiar with it can substantially improve the traveler's experience. While Arabic is the Sultanate's official language, the linguistic landscape in Oman is diverse, reflecting the country's history as a melting pot of cultures and influences.

The majority of Omanis speak Arabic, which comes in a variety of dialects and variations, including the basic Modern basic Arabic (MSA) and regional dialects such as Omani Arabic. MSA is the language of instruction in schools and government, although colloquial dialects are utilized in everyday communication.

Omanis are also very proficient in English, especially in metropolitan areas and among younger generations. English is extensively spoken in business, tourism, and education, making it an invaluable tool for travelers wishing to converse with locals.

Learning a few simple Arabic phrases might help you immerse yourself further into Omani culture. Simple greetings, expressions of gratitude, and simple language for requesting directions or buying meals can improve conversations while also demonstrating respect for local norms.

Oman values nonverbal communication in addition to spoken language. Handshakes are a customary greeting, although some women may prefer not to shake hands with men. Modest clothing is also appreciated, particularly in more traditional places or religious institutions where it is common to be modest.

Signage, official papers, and publications all use the Arabic alphabet for written communication. Oman's number system is also Arabic-based. However, English is commonly utilized in signage for the convenience of international visitors.

Technological improvements have also influenced communication in Oman. With the increased use of smartphones and the internet, communication has become more accessible, with applications and online services providing translation and navigation assistance.

Overall, Oman's linguistic and communication environment reflects the country's diverse cultural heritage as well as its modern, worldwide attitude. A rudimentary understanding of Arabic and respect for Omani customs and etiquette can enhance the traveler's experience and promote meaningful interactions with locals. Whether navigating busy markets in Muscat or touring rural towns in the interior, language and communication are vital tools for connecting with the heart and spirit of Oman.

CHAPTER TWO

Travel Planning

Best Time to Visit

The best time to visit Oman is entirely dependent on the traveler's choices, as each season provides distinct experiences. However, in order to have a pleasant and memorable journey, consider elements such as weather, festivals, and peak travel seasons.

The winter months, November to March, are considered the best time to visit Oman. During this season, temperatures range from 20°C to 30°C (68°F to 86°F), making it excellent for visiting the country's different landscapes, from the coast to the inner mountains. The northern regions, especially those surrounding Muscat and Sohar, have comfortable temperatures and sunny skies, making them ideal for tourism and outdoor sports.

Spring, from March to May, is another great time to visit Oman, as temperatures rise and the landscapes bloom. This season provides an opportunity to see the country's flora and fauna at their peak, as well as engage in cultural events like the Muscat Festival and the Salalah Tourism Festival.

The hottest and least ideal season to visit Oman is during the summer months, which run from June to August. Temperatures can reach 45°C (113°F) or more, making outdoor activities uncomfortable and difficult. However, this is also the Khareef season in Salalah, which brings lush foliage and cool weather, providing a unique opportunity to explore Oman's natural splendor.

Autumn, which runs from September to November, signifies the conclusion of the Khareef season and the start of cooler weather in the rest of the country. This is referred to as the shoulder season since it provides a balance between summer heat and winter throngs. Travelers can enjoy comfortable temperatures and less people, making it an excellent time to visit Oman's various attractions.

It's worth noting that Oman has a largely desert climate, with very little rain all year. While the winter months are often regarded as the ideal time to visit, it is always prudent to check the weather forecast and plan appropriately, particularly if traveling to isolated or hilly places.

Overall, the best time to visit Oman is determined by the traveler's interests and preferences. Oman provides a variety of events throughout the year, including cultural festivals, outdoor adventures, and restful beach vacations.

Budgeting Tips

Budgeting for a trip to Oman can be an important consideration for travelers, as the cost of travel and accommodations can vary widely depending on the season, location, and type of experience. Here are some tips to help travelers manage their budget and make the most of their trip to Oman.

1. **Plan Ahead:** Planning ahead can save travelers time and money. By researching accommodation options, comparing prices, and booking in advance, travelers can often find better deals and secure their preferred accommodation.

2. **Consider Traveling in the Off-Season:** Traveling during the off-season, such as in the shoulder seasons of spring and autumn, or the summer low season, can often result in lower prices for accommodations, flights, and tours. Additionally, popular attractions and sites may be less crowded, allowing for a more leisurely and budget-friendly experience.

3. **Look for Deals and Discounts:** Many hotels and tour operators offer special deals and discounts, especially during the off-season. Travelers should keep an eye out for promotions and offers that may be available.

4. **Choose Budget-Friendly Accommodation:** Oman offers a range of accommodation options to suit different budgets, from luxury hotels and resorts to budget-friendly guesthouses and hostels. Travelers looking to save money can consider staying in more budget-friendly accommodation options, or booking self-catering accommodations to save on dining expenses.

5. **Be Flexible with Transportation:** Traveling around Oman can be costly, especially if renting a car or using taxis. Travelers can save money by using public transportation, sharing rides with other

travelers, or considering carpooling services.

6. **Eat Local:** Eating at local restaurants and markets can be a more affordable option than dining at tourist areas or upscale restaurants. Travelers can also save money by purchasing groceries and preparing meals themselves, especially if staying in self-catering accommodations.

7. **Be Mindful of Entrance Fees and Costs:** Some attractions and sites in Oman may charge entrance fees or have additional costs, such as guided tours or activities. Travelers should be aware of these costs and budget accordingly.

8. **Pack Wisely:** Travelers can save money by packing essentials such as sunscreen, insect repellent, and snacks before arriving in Oman. These items can often be more expensive to purchase at tourist areas.

9. **Consider Travel Insurance:** Travelers should consider purchasing travel insurance to protect themselves against unforeseen events, such as flight cancellations, medical emergencies, or lost baggage. Travel insurance can provide peace of mind and save money in the long run.

10. **Be Open to Alternatives:** Travelers should be open to alternative experiences and options that may be more budget-friendly. This can include staying in less popular areas, choosing cheaper transportation options, or visiting lesser-known attractions.

By following these budgeting tips, travelers can have a more affordable and enjoyable experience in Oman. Whether exploring the country's stunning landscapes, learning about its rich history and culture, or enjoying its delicious cuisine, Oman offers a range of experiences to suit different budgets and interests.

Visa Requirements

Oman's visa requirements are straightforward, and understanding them before you embark on your journey will ensure a smooth entry into the Sultanate. Here's an overview of Oman's visa regulations:

Visa-Free Entry:
Citizens of the GCC (Gulf Cooperation Council) countries (Bahrain, Kuwait, Oman, Qatar, Saudi Arabia, and the United Arab Emirates) enjoy visa-free entry to Oman. Additionally, nationals from more than 100 countries, including the United States, Canada, Australia, New Zealand, and most European Union countries, can obtain a visa on arrival at various entry points, such as Muscat International Airport, Salalah Airport, and land border crossings.

On-Arrival Visa:

For eligible countries, a tourist visa can be obtained upon arrival at the airport or land border. The visa allows a stay of up to 30 days and can be extended for a further 30 days. The fee for a tourist visa on arrival is 20 Omani Rial (approximately 52 USD) for a 10-day visa, 20 Omani Rial (approximately 52 USD) for a 30-day visa, or 20 Omani Rial (approximately 52 USD) for a 1-year multiple-entry visa. Payments can be made in cash or by credit card.

E-Visa:

To streamline the visa application process, Oman also offers an e-visa system for eligible countries. Travelers can apply for an e-visa online through the Royal Oman Police website or via the smartphone app. The e-visa is valid for stays of up to 30 days and is available for single-entry or multiple-entry travel. The fee for an e-visa is 20 Omani Rial (approximately 52 USD).

Tourist Visa:

Travelers from countries not eligible for visa-free entry can apply for a tourist visa, which allows for stays of up to 30 days or 10 days. This type of visa is typically issued for tourism purposes and requires a sponsor or a tour operator.

Visa on Arrival for Cruise Ship Passengers:
Cruise ship passengers arriving at Oman's cruise terminals are eligible for visa-on-arrival services. The visa is valid for a 24-hour stay and costs 5 Omani Rial (approximately 13 USD). Passengers can explore Oman's attractions within the port area or book guided tours organized by the cruise company.

Pre-Arrival Visa:
For travelers who prefer to have their visa arranged before their trip, they can apply for a visa through their nearest Omani consulate or embassy. The visa is valid for a single entry and can be extended if necessary.

Visit Visa: A visit visa is available for travelers seeking a longer stay in Oman, typically for family visits or business purposes. This type of visa allows for stays of up to three months and requires a sponsor, such as a family member or employer, to apply on behalf of the traveler.

Business Visa:
Business travelers can apply for a business visa, which allows for stays of up to three months and is typically issued for business meetings, conferences, or trade events. A sponsor, such as a company or organization, is required to apply on behalf of the traveler.

Student Visa: International students planning to study in Oman can apply for a student visa, which allows for stays of up to three months. This type of visa requires a sponsor, such as a university or educational institution, to apply on behalf of the student.

Employment Visa:
Travelers planning to work in Oman must obtain an employment visa, which allows for stays of up to three months and requires a sponsor, such

as an employer, to apply on behalf of the traveler.

Residency Visas:
Those planning to work, study, or live in Oman for an extended period will require a residency visa. The requirements and process for obtaining a residency visa differ depending on the individual's circumstances and the type of visa required.

It is important to note that visa regulations are subject to change, and travelers should always check the latest requirements and procedures before traveling. Additionally, travelers are advised to adhere to local laws and customs during their stay in Oman, and failure to comply may result in fines or deportation. Overall, Oman's visa regulations are designed to facilitate tourism and encourage visitors to explore the Sultanate's diverse landscapes, rich history, and vibrant culture.

Engaging a travel agent can be beneficial for a trip to Oman:

- **Research:** Look for travel agencies specializing in Oman and read reviews.

- **Contact:** Reach out to a travel agent via email, phone, or in person.

- **Provide Information:** Share travel details, preferences, and requirements.

- **Review and Confirm:** Review the itinerary and costs, ask questions, and confirm the booking.

By working with a travel agent, travelers can receive professional help and ensure a smooth experience in Oman.

Itinerary Planning

Itinerary planning is an essential aspect of any trip to Oman, as it helps travelers make the most of their time and experience the best that the Sultanate has to offer.

When planning an itinerary for Oman, it's important to consider the following factors:

Duration of Stay: The length of stay in Oman will determine the scope and flexibility of the itinerary. Travelers should allow for enough time to explore the various regions and attractions at a leisurely pace.

Mode of Transportation: Whether traveling by car, bus, or plane, the chosen mode of transportation will influence the itinerary. Travelers should consider travel times, distances, and accessibility when planning their routes.

Accommodation: Choosing the right accommodation is crucial to the overall travel experience. Travelers should research and book accommodations that meet their budget, preferences, and travel style.

Must-See Attractions: Oman offers a wealth of attractions, from ancient forts and castles to pristine beaches and rugged mountains. Travelers should prioritize must-see attractions based on their interests and preferences.

Cultural Experiences: Oman's rich culture and heritage are best experienced through traditional markets, museums, and cultural festivals. Travelers should include cultural experiences in their itinerary to gain a deeper understanding of Oman's history and traditions.

Outdoor Activities: Outdoor enthusiasts can explore Oman's diverse landscapes through hiking, camping, diving, and other outdoor activities. Travelers should plan their itineraries to include these activities, ensuring an adventurous and active trip.

Local Cuisine: Oman's cuisine is a reflection of its diverse culture and history. Travelers should make time to sample local dishes and visit traditional eateries to savor the flavors of Oman.

Rest and Relaxation: Traveling can be exhausting, so it's important to include time for rest and relaxation in the itinerary. Travelers should schedule downtime to recharge and unwind, ensuring a balanced and enjoyable trip.

Flexibility: Travelers should be flexible and open to adjustments during their trip. Unexpected changes, such as weather conditions or unexpected delays, may require itinerary adjustments. Having a flexible mindset can help travelers make the most of their time in Oman.

Budget: Setting a budget is essential for itinerary planning. Travelers should consider transportation, accommodation, activities, meals, and souvenirs when budgeting for their trip. Being mindful of expenses can help travelers make informed decisions and avoid overspending.

Language and Communication: English is widely spoken in Oman, especially in tourist areas. However, knowing a few basic Arabic phrases can be helpful when interacting with locals. Travelers should consider learning basic greetings, phrases, and numbers to facilitate communication.

Cultural Sensitivity: Oman is a Muslim-majority country with conservative cultural norms. Travelers should dress modestly, especially when visiting religious sites or rural areas. Being respectful of local customs and traditions can help travelers avoid cultural misunderstandings and show appreciation for Omani culture.

Health Precautions: Travelers should take necessary health precautions when visiting Oman, such as staying hydrated, using sunscreen, and avoiding food and water that may be contaminated. It's also advisable to bring any necessary medications and have travel insurance that covers medical emergencies.

Emergency Contacts: Before traveling to Oman, travelers should make a list of emergency contacts, including local authorities, embassy or consulate information, and contacts for their accommodations. Having this information readily available can be helpful in case of emergencies.

Creating a well-thought-out itinerary for Oman requires careful planning and consideration of various factors. By planning ahead and being flexible, travelers can ensure a rewarding and memorable experience in Oman.

Safety and Health

When visiting Oman, it is critical to ensure your safety and stay healthy. The country is typically safe, with low crime and a friendly population.

To ensure a worry-free trip, travelers should constantly exercise caution and follow safety recommendations.

Personal Safety

Personal Safety: Travelers should be cautious of their things and avoid flaunting valuables in public. Petty theft can occur in busy settings, so keep your belongings safe.

Road Safety: Oman's roads can be difficult to manage, especially in remote areas. Travelers should drive carefully, follow speed limits, and use seatbelts. Rental vehicles should be inspected for safety features, and drivers should be conversant with Oman's driving restrictions.

Outdoor Activities: Oman's diverse environments provide a variety of outdoor activities such as trekking, diving, and desert safaris. Travelers should engage in these activities with licensed operators that follow safety rules and norms.

Weather Conditions: Temperatures in Oman can reach 45°C (113°F) in the summer. Travelers should stay hydrated, apply sunscreen, and wear protective clothes, especially when participating in outdoor activities.

Cultural Sensitivity: Oman is a conservative country, and visitors should adhere to local customs and traditions. It is recommended that you dress modestly, especially while visiting holy locations, and avoid making public shows of affection.

Health

immunizations: Depending on their travel goals and medical history, travelers should keep up with normal immunizations and consider Hepatitis A, Typhoid, and Hepatitis B vaccines.

Food and Water: While Oman's tap water is typically safe to drink, bottled water is commonly available and advised, particularly in rural regions. Travelers should also avoid eating undercooked or uncooked foods, instead opting for hot, freshly prepared dishes.

Sun Protection: Oman's hot sun can cause sunburn and heatstroke. Travelers should use high-SPF sunscreen, wear protective clothes, and seek shade during the warmest hours of the day.

Mosquito-Borne Diseases: While Oman is not a malaria-risk country, visitors should take precautions against mosquito bites, including as using insect repellent, sleeping beneath mosquito nets, and wearing long sleeves and pants.

Medical Facilities: While Oman boasts advanced medical facilities in its cities, medical services may be restricted in rural areas. Travelers should carry travel insurance that covers medical emergencies and be prepared to seek medical attention if necessary.

Medication: Travelers should pack an adequate supply of any prescribed drugs, as well as a copy of their prescription, in case they need to refill it while in Oman.

Emergency Contacts: Travelers should save a list of emergency contacts, such as local authorities, embassy or consulate information, and contact information for their lodging.

Stay Informed: Travelers should be aware of any health advisories or travel alerts for Oman and be prepared to change their trip plans appropriately.

Travelers who follow these safety and health advice can have a safe and happy stay in Oman.

CHAPTER THREE

Transportation

Air Travel

Oman has a well-developed air travel infrastructure, with several major airports. Here's what you need to know about air travel to and within Oman:

Major Airports: Muscat International Airport, which is the nation's capital city of Muscat, is the principal international airport in Oman. It is Oman's major airport and the primary entry point into the nation. The airport is well-equipped with contemporary amenities, such as restaurants, lounges, and duty-free stores.

Regional Airports: Oman has several regional airports that is available for smaller cities and towns. These airports include Salalah Airport in Salalah, Sohar Airport in Sohar, and Duqm

Airport in Duqm. These airports offer domestic and limited international flights, providing convenient access to various regions of Oman.

Airlines: Oman is connected to major cities across the globe by a number of international airlines that provide flights to and from the nation. The national airline of Oman, Oman Air, provides service to locations in Europe, Asia, and the Middle East. Etihad Airways, Emirates, and Qatar Airways are among the other carriers that fly to and from Oman.

Domestic Flights: Domestic flights within Oman are operated by Oman Air and other regional airlines. These flights connect Muscat with other major cities in Oman, including Salalah, Sohar, and Duqm. Domestic flights are a convenient way to travel within Oman, especially for business travelers and tourists exploring multiple regions.

Visa Requirements: Visitors to Oman must obtain a visa before traveling to the country, unless they are citizens of visa-exempt countries. Most visitors can obtain a tourist visa upon arrival at Muscat International Airport, valid for a stay of up to 30 days. However, it is recommended to check visa requirements and apply for a visa in advance to avoid any issues.

Transportation from Airport: Upon arrival at Muscat International Airport, visitors can choose from various transportation options to reach their final destination. These include taxis, private car rentals, and hotel shuttles. Additionally, the airport is served by public buses that connect the airport with the city center and other destinations.

Airport Services: A variety of amenities and services are available at Muscat International Airport to guarantee a convenient and enjoyable travel experience. These consist of baggage handling, currency exchange, and help for travelers with specific requirements. There are also lots of different restaurants and retail establishments at the airport.

COVID-19 Precautions: Due to the existence of COVID-19 pandemic, travelers to Oman are required to follow certain health and safety protocols. This may include wearing masks, practicing social distancing, and providing proof of vaccination or a negative COVID-19 test result. It is recommended to check the latest travel advisories and regulations before planning a trip.

Air travel to and within Oman is efficient and convenient, Oman's airports and airlines ensures a comfortable and hassle-free travel experience.

Public / Local Transport Options

Public transportation in Oman is an integral part of daily life for many Omanis and visitors alike. Oman's government has invested significantly in infrastructure, resulting in a well-organized system of buses, taxis, and ferries that cater to the needs of both locals and tourists.

The Oman National Transport Company (Mwasalat) operates the country's bus services, which run on a variety of routes across cities, towns, and regions. Mwasalat's fleet of modern, air-conditioned buses are equipped with Wi-Fi, providing a comfortable and convenient option for travelers to explore the country's diverse landscapes.

Taxis are a common sight in Oman, offering a flexible mode of transportation for individuals and groups. Taxis can be found at designated taxi stands, outside hotels, and hailed on the streets. They are usually metered, but it's wise to agree on the fare beforehand. Taxis can also be booked through mobile apps or hotel concierges for added convenience.

Ferries are essential for those wanting to explore Oman's islands or travel between the mainland and the Musandam Peninsula. The National

Ferries Company operates ferry services, providing a scenic way to travel and offering the opportunity to witness Oman's stunning coastal views. Masirah Island, known for its pristine beaches and wildlife, is just one example of a ferry destination worth exploring.

Traveling between cities is made easy with Oman's bus services, taxis, and rental cars. The Sultanate's major cities are well-connected by highways and roads, making it simple to navigate and explore the country's diverse regions.

Prior to embarking on your journey, consider researching your options and planning your routes accordingly. Public transportation schedules and routes can be found online or obtained from local tourism offices. For those seeking a more flexible travel experience, car rentals are readily available and provide the freedom to explore at your own pace.

The cost of public transportation in Oman is generally reasonable. Bus fares are affordable, and taxis offer metered rates. Additionally, ferry prices are competitive, especially considering the scenic views and convenience they provide.

Oman's public transportation is accessible to all, including individuals with disabilities. Buses and taxis are equipped to accommodate individuals with mobility impairments, and ferry services are designed to cater to the needs of all passengers.

Oman's public transportation system is efficient and reliable.

CHAPTER FOUR

Accommodations

Hotel Options and Budget Lodging
Luxury Resorts

The Chedi Muscat (Muscat): The Chedi is a five-star luxury resort located in the capital city of Muscat, surrounded by gorgeous gardens and tranquil waterways. It provides a variety of exquisite rooms and villas, all with modern conveniences and traditional Omani design. The prices range from $300 to $1,000 each night.

Six Senses Zighy Bay (Musandam Peninsula): Six Senses Zighy Bay, located in a secluded harbor on the Musandam Peninsula, is an ultra-luxurious resort with private pool villas and breathtaking mountain views. Prices start at $700 per night.

Boutique Hotels

Al Bustan Palace, A Ritz-Carlton Hotel (Muscat): Al Bustan Palace, which has a view of the Gulf of Oman, combines contemporary grandeur with traditional Omani architecture. The price rates for each night vary from $200 to $700.

Desert Nights Camp (Wahiba Sands): Located in the heart of the Wahiba Sands desert, Desert Nights Camp has luxurious tented accommodations with desert views. Prices start from $200 per night.

Business Hotels

InterContinental Muscat (Muscat): Situated in the heart of the city, InterContinental Muscat has convenient access to the business district and major attractions. Prices range from $100 to $400 per night.

Crowne Plaza Resort Salalah (Salalah): Located in Salalah, Crowne Plaza Resort has comfortable rooms and business amenities. Prices start from $80 per night.

Budget Hotels

Tulip Inn Downtown Muscat (Muscat): Situated in the city center, Tulip Inn offers affordable accommodations with easy access to attractions. Prices range from $50 to $100 per night.

Al Falaj Hotel (Muscat): A budget-friendly option in Muscat, Al Falaj Hotel provides comfortable rooms at affordable rates. Prices start from $50 per night.

Serviced Apartments

Fraser Suites Muscat (Muscat): It is situated in the nation's capital, has large, fully equipped suites with contemporary conveniences. Prices range from $150 to $300 per night.

Somerset Panorama Muscat (Muscat): The efficient and cozy apartments at Somerset Panorama Muscat are ideal for long stays because of their proximity to the airport. The starting price each night is $100.

Resorts

Resorts in Oman are a luxurious and immersive experience, Oman's resorts provide a tranquil retreat where guests can relax and recharge.

Beach Resorts

Shangri-La Barr Al Jissah Resort & Spa (Muscat): The magnificent Shangri-La Barr Al Jissah Resort & Spa in Muscat is tucked away in a quiet harbor close to the city. It is a luxurious seaside getaway. This resort is a peaceful haven with its lush gardens, infinity pools, and private beach. Numerous eating options, including both traditional and international Omani cuisine, are available at the resort.

Al Baleed Resort Salalah by Anantara (Salalah): located near Salalah on the Arabian Sea coast, combines opulence with traditional Omani hospitality. The resort features traditional features like arched walkways and ornamental screens in its construction, which draws inspiration from the Dhofar region surrounding it.

Mountain Resorts

Anantara Al Jabal Al Akhdar Resort (Al Jabal Al Akhdar): located 2,000 meters above sea level in the Al Hajar Mountains, presents stunning views of the surrounding canyons and valleys. The resort is well-known for its infinity pool, which overlooks the cliffs, as well as its exquisite spa and wellness center.

Alila Jabal Akhdar (Al Jabal Al Akhdar): Another mountain retreat in Al Jabal Al Akhdar, Alila Jabal Akhdar is a serene escape from the hustle and bustle of everyday life. Guests can enjoy outdoor activities such as hiking, mountain biking, and stargazing.

Desert Resorts

Desert Nights Camp (Wahiba Sands): Desert Nights Camp, located in the center of the Wahiba Sands desert, is a one-of-a-kind glamping experience. Guests stay in classic Bedouin tents outfitted with modern facilities and comfy furnishings. The camp provides desert tours, camel rides, and cultural activities.

Anantara Qasr Al Sarab Desert Resort (Liwa): Anantara Qasr Al Sarab Desert Resort is an exquisite desert hideaway, tucked away among the towering dunes of the Rub' al Khali desert. The resort's opulent rooms come furnished with contemporary conveniences, and its style is reminiscent of classic Arabian architecture.

CHAPTER FIVE

Dining and Cuisine

Popular Restaurant and Local Dishes

Oman's culinary scene is a delightful blend of traditional flavors and international influences. Here's a captivating overview of popular restaurants and must-try local dishes:

Popular Restaurants

Bin Ateeq: Located in Muscat, Bin Ateeq is a renowned restaurant that specializes in traditional Omani cuisine. With its warm and welcoming ambiance, it features dishes made with fresh local ingredients and traditional cooking methods. Signature dishes include Mashuai (slow-cooked spiced rice with tender roasted lamb) and Shuwa (marinated meat cooked underground).

Bait Al Luban: Bait Al Luban is a quaint eatery located in the center of Muttrah Souq in Muscat, well-known for its delicious Omani fish specialties. Freshly caught seafood and shellfish cooked with regional Omani spices and flavors are served to diners. Sayadieh, or spiced fish with rice, and Hammour Machboos, or grilled hammour fish served with rice, are two must-try meals.

Ubhar: Ubhar, which is housed in a historic structure in Muscat's Old Town, serves modern Omani cuisine. Both residents and visitors enjoy the restaurant's creative menu and elegant atmosphere. Omani Lamb Tagine and Omani Chicken Kabsa are two dishes that symbolize the unique tastes and culinary customs of the area.

Kargeen Caffe: Kargeen Caffe, located in Muscat's lovely garden setting, is a popular venue for outdoor dining and traditional Omani cuisine. The comprehensive menu include Omani specialties such as Omani Chicken Majboos (spiced rice with soft chicken) and

Omani Halwa (a sweet dessert prepared with sugar, rosewater, and nuts).

Dukanah Café: Located in the picturesque village of Misfat Al Abriyeen in Al Dakhiliyah Governorate, Dukanah Café. Visitors can sample traditional dishes such as Majboos, Saloona (vegetable stew), and Mishkak (grilled meat skewers) while enjoying panoramic views of the surrounding mountains.

Must-Try Local Dishes

Omani Shuwa: Shuwa is a traditional Omani dish consisting of marinated meat (usually lamb or goat) cooked slowly underground for several hours. The result is tender, flavorful meat with aromatic spices and herbs, served with fragrant rice and traditional bread.

Maqbous: Maqbous is a popular Omani rice dish cooked with a variety of spices, vegetables, and meat (often chicken or fish). It's similar to biryani but with its own unique Omani twist, featuring flavors such as saffron, cardamom, and dried limes.

Halwa: Omani Halwa is a sweet dessert made from sugar, rosewater, and nuts. It has a sticky, gelatinous texture and is often flavored with saffron, cardamom, and nuts. It's a popular treat served during special occasions and celebrations.

Mashuai: Mashuai is a traditional Omani dish consisting of spiced rice topped with tender roasted lamb or goat. The rice is cooked with a blend of spices and served with a flavorful broth made from the meat juices.

Madrouba: Madrouba is a hearty Omani stew with chicken, rice, and vegetables. It's meticulously cooked until the ingredients are delicate and the tastes blend, resulting in a satisfying dish.

Oman would certainly please your taste buds and leave you longing for more.

Eating Etiquette

Eating etiquette in Oman is strongly rooted in tradition and culture, reflecting the country's long history and numerous influences. Visitors should respect and appreciate the Omani way of life by following specific norms when dining in a local diner or a luxurious restaurant. Here are some important things to remember when dining in Oman:

Use Your Right Hand: The right hand is considered clean and suitable for handling food and utensils. The left hand is typically reserved for personal hygiene and should not be used for eating or handling food.

Eating with tools: While Omani cuisine is traditionally eaten with the right hand, many modern restaurants and hotels offer tools like forks and spoons. When using utensils, use the right hand and avoid handling food directly with the left.

Sharing Food: In Omani culture, kindness and sharing are highly valued, particularly when it comes to food. When dining with others, food are typically served family-style, with everyone taking a part from the shared plates.

Dining with Guests: If you are asked to an Omani home for a dinner, accept it gracefully and attend on time. Guests should follow the host's lead in terms of seating arrangements and dining decorum.

Fasting During Ramadan: Muslims in Oman fast from dawn to sunset. Visitors should be mindful of this and avoid eating, drinking, or smoking in public during daytime hours in order to honor people fasting.

Alcohol Consumption: Oman is largely Muslim, hence alcohol usage is restricted. While some hotels and restaurants sell alcohol, it is crucial to respect local traditions and avoid excessive drinking in public places.

Tipping: Tipping is optional in Oman, but it is appreciated. It is traditional to leave a little gratuity for good service, usually between 10-15% of the cost.

Recognizing the Host: After the meal, it is customary to thank the host for their kindness. This can be accomplished by simply saying "shukran" (thank you) or giving a small gift.

Eating Times: The main meal of the day in Oman is usually eaten in the afternoon or evening. Restaurants and cafes typically begin serving lunch about noon and dinner around 7:00 p.m. or later.

Dining at Traditional Restaurants: For a genuinely authentic dining experience, travelers can choose traditional Omani restaurants or "local" cafes. These eateries serve traditional Omani cuisine, frequently in a communal setting.

By following these standards, tourists can have a courteous and pleasurable eating experience that honors Omani culture and hospitality.

CHAPTER SIX

Attractions and Activities

Must-See Sites

Let's explore some of the top destinations that should be on every traveler's itinerary when visiting this enchanting country.

1. Muscat - The Capital City
Muscat, the capital city of Oman, is a vibrant metropolis located between the mountains and the sea. Here, you can explore the iconic Sultan Qaboos Grand Mosque, stroll through the historic Muttrah Souq, and marvel at the imposing Al Jalali and Al Mirani forts.

2. Wahiba Sands - Desert Adventures
For a taste of the Arabian Desert, head to Wahiba Sands, also known as Sharqiya Sands. Embark on a thrilling desert safari, where you can ride camels over towering sand dunes, camp

under the starlit sky, and experience the timeless allure of Bedouin culture.

3. Nizwa - Cultural Gem
Nizwa, the former capital of Oman, is renowned for its rich heritage and traditional architecture. Explore the imposing Nizwa Fort, witness the ancient art of falaj irrigation systems.

4. Jabal Akhdar - The Green Mountain
Escape the heat and explore the cool heights of Jabal Akhdar, Oman's stunning Green Mountain. Trek through terraced gardens, explore picturesque villages, and take in panoramic views of the rugged landscape below.

5. Salalah - The Land of Frankincense
In the south of Oman lies Salalah, a coastal city steeped in history and natural beauty. Discover the ancient ruins of Sumhuram, stroll along pristine beaches, and visit the vibrant Al Husn Souq for a taste of local culture.

6. Wadi Shab - Oasis of Tranquility

Wadi Shab offers a unique blend of adventure and serenity. Hike through narrow gorges, swim in crystal-clear pools, and marvel at the stunning waterfalls hidden within the canyon.

7. Ras Al Jinz - Turtle Watching
Nature lovers shouldn't miss the opportunity to witness the nesting ritual of endangered green turtles at Ras Al Jinz. Guided tours are available to observe these magnificent creatures in their natural habitat.

8. Jebel Shams - The Grand Canyon of Oman
For awe-inspiring vistas and rugged terrain, Jebel Shams, the highest peak in the Hajar Mountains, is a must-visit destination. Trek along the edge of the canyon for breathtaking views that rival those of the Grand Canyon.

9. Sur - Seafaring Heritage
Sur, a coastal town steeped in maritime history, offers a glimpse into Oman's seafaring heritage. Explore the ancient dhow shipyards, stroll along

the picturesque waterfront, and witness traditional boat-building techniques firsthand.

10. Al Hoota Cave - Underground Wonder
Delve into the mysterious depths of Al Hoota Cave, one of Oman's most impressive natural wonders. Explore illuminated caverns, marvel at ancient stalactites and stalagmites, and learn about the geological significance of this subterranean marvel.

11. Bahla - UNESCO World Heritage Site
Step back in time as you explore the ancient mud-brick fortifications of Bahla, a UNESCO World Heritage Site. Wander through labyrinthine corridors, admire intricate carvings, and soak in the rich history of this well-preserved fortress.

12. Jebel Akhdar - The Green Jewel
Jebel Akhdar, or the Green Mountain, beckons with its terraced farms, fruit orchards, and cool mountain air. Enjoy leisurely walks amidst blooming roses, sample fresh local produce, and

unwind in the tranquil surroundings of this verdant oasis.

13. **Al Sawadi Beach** - Coastal Retreat
For sun, sand, and relaxation, head to Al Sawadi Beach, a pristine stretch of coastline fringed by palm trees. Whether you're swimming, snorkeling, or simply soaking up the sun, this idyllic beach offers the perfect escape from the hustle and bustle of city life.

14. **Sohar** - Historical Port City
Sohar, once a bustling port city on the ancient frankincense trade route, is steeped in history and culture.

15. **Ras Al Hadd** - Coastal Paradise
Ras Al Hadd is a tranquil coastal village renowned for its pristine beaches and abundant marine life. Explore coral reefs teeming with colorful fish, watch dolphins frolic in the azure waters, and unwind amidst the natural beauty of this coastal paradise.

Adventure Activities

Adventure seekers have an abundance of options in Oman, where they can engage in a wide range of exhilarating activities against the stunning backdrop of the country's rough terrain. Oman provides travelers looking for adventure with a wide range of heart-pounding adventures, from thrilling desert safaris to challenging mountain hikes.

Take a trek among the stunning peaks of the *Al Hajar Mountains* to start your experience. Put on your boots and embark on the strenuous paths that meander through breathtaking gorges, imposing cliffs, and lush wadis. You will be rewarded with breathtaking sweeping vistas of the neighboring valleys and villages below as you navigate the rugged terrain. The tallest peak in Oman, Jebel Shams, would make you experience breathtaking views into the breathtaking Wadi Ghul, also referred to as the

Grand Canyon of Arabia. Don't pass up the chance to climb it.

For those who have a thirst for water sports, spend a day kayaking or paddleboarding on the ***Musandam Peninsula's pristine waterways***. Cruise the craggy coast, discovering undiscovered coves, deserted beaches, and sheer sea cliffs. As you go through the calm waters of the Arabian Gulf, watch out for playful dolphins and vibrant marine life.

Take a thrilling dune bashing journey into the ***Wahiba Sands*** for the ultimate desert adventure. Climb into a 4x4 vehicle and buckle up while your knowledgeable driver expertly drives through the tall sand dunes. As you rocket up and down the steep inclines and weave through the never-ending sea of sand, experience the surge of excitement. Before retiring to a traditional Bedouin camp for an evening of stargazing and storytelling beneath the sparkling desert sky, stop to watch the sun set over the horizon.

Take to the skies with a tandem paragliding or paramotoring excursion over the steep slopes of *Jebel Akhdar* or the seaside cliffs of Dhofar for a totally unique experience. Take in breathtaking aerial views of Oman's magnificent landscapes below as you soar through the skies like a bird.

Oman has an abundance of adventure activities that are sure to make your heart race and leave you with lifelong memories.

Shopping Destinations

A multitude of shopping places with an array of treasures waiting to be discovered in Oman's busy markets and contemporary retail centers. Oman offers a wide range of shopping experiences to suit every taste and inclination, from posh malls featuring international brands to traditional souks bursting with regional handicrafts.

In the center of Muscat sits **Muttrah Souq**, one of the most famous shopping locations in Oman. This centuries-old market is a maze of tiny lanes crammed with vendors selling anything which could be jewelry and antiques to spices and textiles.

The **Oman Avenues Mall** and **Muscat Grand Mall** are two of the city's upmarket malls, catering to people looking for a more contemporary shopping experience. Shoppers can peruse an extensive array of global brands, upscale boutiques, and fine dining establishments, all contained within modern, air-conditioned buildings. You could be looking for electronics, gourmet food, or luxury clothing, these malls has a convenient and welcoming shopping experience.

Outside of Muscat, the city of **Nizwa** is well known for its historic souks, which give visitors a chance to witness the genuine allure of Omani trade. The vibrant Nizwa Souq has a wide range of products, such as handcrafted fabrics, spices, and pottery. Explore the old market, bargain with local vendors, and find one-of-a-kind items to bring home as treasured keepsakes of their trip to Oman.

Salalah, a city in southern Oman, has a distinctive shopping environment of its own, with busy souks and contemporary malls. Persons can peruse a wide range of products at the bustling Salalah Souk, including fresh fruit, spices, and traditional Omani handicrafts. A more modern shopping experience is provided by the Salalah Gardens Mall, which has a variety of stores, eateries, and entertainment venues to choose from.

Sur is a good location for anyone looking for genuine Omans handicrafts and souvenirs. Dhow building is a centuries-old tradition in Sur, and tourists may tour the city's shipyards and workshops to see master craftspeople building these ancient wooden boats by hand. Furthermore, visitors may find a wide range of locally produced items in Sur's busy souks, including as ceramics, textiles, and silverware, giving them the ideal chance to buy thoughtful and distinctive mementos.

CHAPTER SEVEN

Family Travel

Family-Friendly Attractions

Oman is a family-friendly location with a variety of attractions that appeal to people of all ages. From breathtaking beaches and natural treasures to cultural icons and family-friendly activities.

Beaches: Oman's coastline is dotted with magnificent beaches with turquoise waters and gentle sands, ideal for families looking to spend the day sunbathing, swimming, and relaxing. Popular family beaches include Muscat's Al Qurum Beach, Salalah Beach in the south, and the Musandam Peninsula's scenic beaches.

Wadis: Oman's wadis, or natural water pools, are great for family activities. Wadis like Wadi Bani Khalid and Wadi Shab allow you to swim, picnic, and explore Oman's natural splendor.

Desert Adventures: Families can go on camel rides, dune bashing, and camp beneath the stars. The Wahiba Sands and Rub' al Khali deserts are popular destinations for families looking to experience Oman's desert culture.

Historical sites in Oman, such as Nizwa Fort, Jabreen Castle, and Bahla Fort, illustrate the country's rich history. Families may explore these ancient sites, learn about Oman's history, and take guided excursions.

Cultural Experiences: Traditional performances, excursions to souks (markets), and participation in cultural workshops allow families to immerse themselves in Oman's diverse culture. Families especially enjoy Muscat's Muttrah Souq and Nizwa Souq.

Dolphin Watching: Families can go on dolphin-watching cruises in Oman's coastal waters and see joyful dolphins frolicking in the sea. The waters surrounding Muscat and the Musandam

Peninsula are well-known for their dolphin populations.

Water Parks: Oman has various water parks, including Al Hoota Cave Park and Muscat Aqua Park, where families may enjoy water slides, wave pools, and other water-related activities.

Museums: Oman includes various museums for families, including the National Museum of Oman, the Bait Al Zubair Museum, and the Oman Children's Museum. These museums provide interactive exhibits and educational events that are appropriate for all ages.

Wildlife: Families may discover Oman's unique wildlife by visiting nature reserves and animal sanctuaries. The Ras Al Jinz Turtle Reserve is notable for its nesting turtles, while the Arabian Oryx Sanctuary protects the endangered Arabian Oryx.

Eco-Tourism: Oman is dedicated to maintaining its natural environment, and families can enjoy eco-tourism activities like bird viewing, trekking, and camping. The Dhofar region and the Jebel Akhdar Mountains are notable ecotourism attractions.

Oman Aquarium: Located in Muscat, the Oman Aquarium is a popular family attraction that provides a unique underwater experience. Families may experience the Arabian Sea's diverse aquatic life, which includes sharks, rays, and vibrant coral reefs.

Al Hoota Cave: It islocated in the foothills of Jebel Shams, is one of Oman's most beautiful natural attractions. Families can take a guided tour through the cave's spectacular chambers, which feature stunning stalactites and stalagmites.

Childrens park: Oman has various children's parks where families can participate in outdoor activities and play on playgrounds. Picnics and family gatherings are ideal at parks such as

Qurum Park in Muscat and Shati Al-Qurm Park in Al Qurum.

Bimmah Sinkhole, often known as the "Hawaiian Hole," is a natural wonder located in Hawiyat Najm Park. Families can swim in the sinkhole's crystal-clear waters to cool off from the hot weather.

Water Sports: Oman's coastal waters provide chances for water sports such as snorkeling, diving, and kayaking. Families may discover Oman's beautiful underwater world and participate in activities appropriate for all ages.

Horseback Riding: Families may go horseback riding across Oman's picturesque landscape, discovering mountain trails and seaside paths. Horseback riding tours are accessible in a variety of locations, including the Salalah and Jebel Akhdar areas.

Traditional Omani Experiences: Families can become immersed in Omani culture by visiting traditional events and festivals. The Muscat Festival and Salalah Tourism Festival provide fantastic chances for families to learn about Omani hospitality and culture.

Souvenir Shopping: Local markets and souks provide a variety of distinctive Omani souvenirs for families to purchase. Handcrafted items like pottery, linens, and silverware are excellent memories from their journey to Oman.

Educational Tours: Oman provides educational tours and workshops for families who want to learn about the country's history and culture. The Bait Al Zubair Museum in Muscat and the Oman Children's Museum are excellent venues to learn about Oman's heritage.

Picnic locations: Oman's gorgeous landscapes offer several picnic locations for families to spend the day outdoors. Wadis like Wadi Bani Khalid and Wadi Shab are popular destinations for families seeking to unwind and enjoy the great outdoors.

CHAPTER EIGHT

Business Travel

Business Etiquette

Understanding and respecting local customs and cultural norms is essential for doing business in Oman. Travelers who follow proper business etiquette can form strong relationships, build trust, and execute successful commercial transactions. Here are some important business etiquette guidelines to bear in mind:

Formal and Conservative Atire: Omani business clothing is traditional and modest. Men should wear suits or traditional Omani garb, while ladies should dress conservatively and cover their arms and legs. Bright colors and showy accessories should be avoided as they can be perceived as excessive.

Greetings: Greetings are essential in Omani culture and are frequently followed by handshakes. It is vital to greet with the right hand because the left hand is considered unclean. Men should wait for women to extend their hands for a handshake, although some women may not do so in a professional atmosphere.

Language: Arabic is Oman's official language, however English is commonly spoken, particularly in commercial contexts. It is appropriate to greet individuals with the Arabic greeting "As-salamu alaykum," which means "peace be upon you." Additionally, it is traditional to address people using their titles, such as "Dr.," "Mr.," or "Mrs./Ms.," followed by their last name.

Business Meetings: Punctuality is vital in Oman, therefore come on time for meetings. Meetings may begin with small talk, so be prepared to participate in informal discussion before getting into business. Prepare to negotiate, as the Omani business culture encourages consensus and compromise.

Communication Style: The Omani business culture is subtle and polite. To avoid direct confrontation, people typically employ courteous words and soothing platitudes. It is critical to have a respectful and calm tone during business meetings.

Gift-giving: Gift-giving is a frequent tradition in Omani business culture, and it should be done thoughtfully. Gifts should be modest and given with the right or both hands. It is usual to deny a present at first as a display of humility, but it is polite to accept it after the offer is repeated.

Business cards: Business cards are exchanged during first meetings and should be presented with the right or both hands. It is appropriate to read the business card before placing it in a pocket or cardholder.

Decision-making Process: Decision-making in Omani corporate culture is frequently consensus-based and can be time-consuming. Be patient and avoid forcing business partners to make rapid judgments.

Respect for Authority: In Omani corporate culture, respect for authority and hierarchy is highly valued. It is critical to show reverence and respect to senior members of organizations and government officials.

Dining Etiquette: In Omani business meetings, it's necessary to follow proper dining etiquette.
Follow your host's lead in terms of seating arrangements and meal selection. Eat with utensils rather than your hands, unless the item is typically served that way.

Public Behavior: Omani tradition discourages public expressions of affection.
Respect local norms and traditions, and avoid actions that could be interpreted as rude or offensive.

Business hours: Business hours in Oman might vary, with government agencies normally open from Sunday to Thursday.

Be aware of local holidays and observances, as commercial activity may be restricted during these periods.

Resilience and Adaptability: Oman is a diversified and dynamic country where business conditions can change quickly.

Be resilient and adaptive to unexpected events, and be ready to change your business approach as needed.

Understanding Islamic Traditions: Islam has a huge impact on Omani culture and economic practices.

Be mindful of Islamic traditions, such as fasting during Ramadan, and schedule your company activities accordingly.

Networking and Relationship Building: Omani corporate culture values strong partnerships and trust.
Attending social events and cultural gatherings might help you network and create relationships.

Environmental Awareness: Oman prioritizes environmental sustainability and conservation activities.
When conducting business, consider environmental principles such as waste reduction and resource conservation.

By following these business etiquette guidelines, visitors to Oman can navigate the business world with confidence, respect, and success.

Meeting Facilities

Oman, with its blend of contemporary infrastructure and ancient charm, has a profusion of meeting spaces to suit a wide range of demands and preferences. Whether you're planning a small business meeting, a corporate conference, or a large-scale event, Oman's broad range of venues is sure to meet and surpass your expectations. Here's a closer look at the interesting meeting facilities that Oman has to offer.

Hotels: For example, The Chedi Muscat is a premium hotel in Muscat with a variety of meeting and event spaces. The hotel has a variety of amenities, including elegant boardrooms and large ballrooms, all equipped with cutting-edge technology and services. Its tranquil beachfront setting and excellent service make it an ideal destination for corporate meetings, seminars, and social events.

Convention Centers: Example: Oman Convention and Exhibition Centre (OCEC): Located in Muscat, OCEC is Oman's finest conference and exposition complex. With its world-class facilities and adaptable areas, it can accommodate large-scale conferences, exhibits, and trade displays. Its accessible location and closeness to major hotels make it an attractive venue for national and international events.

Business Hubs: Example: Knowledge Oasis Muscat (KOM): KOM, located in Muscat, is a high-tech business park that includes multiple business centers, co-working spaces, and meeting rooms. Its cutting-edge facilities and skilled support services make it a perfect site for startups, entrepreneurs, and established enterprises to hold meetings, workshops, and seminars.

Event Spaces: For example, Ghubrah Beach Park, located near Muscat, provides a gorgeous and spacious outdoor setting for business events and social gatherings. With its rich foliage and tranquil seaside environment, it's ideal for conducting outdoor conferences, team-building activities, and special events.

Cultural Venues: Example: Royal Opera House Muscat (ROHM): ROHM, based in Muscat, is Oman's premier cultural facility, hosting a range of concerts and events. Its beautiful design and cutting-edge facilities make it a one-of-a-kind and unforgettable setting for business gatherings, product launches, and gala dinners.

Luxury Resorts: For example, consider Al Bustan Palace, a Ritz-Carlton hotel: Al Bustan Palace is a luxury resort located between the Al Hajar Mountains and the Gulf of Oman. It provides beautiful conference and event facilities. Its exquisite ballrooms, seaside settings, and world-class amenities make it an ideal location for high-profile meetings, incentives, and corporate retreats.

Country Clubs in the Al Hajar Mountains: Nestled amidst the majestic Al Hajar Mountains, the Jebel Akhdar Country Club offers a tranquil setting for corporate meetings and retreats. Its gorgeous setting and luxury amenities make it a great venue for corporate functions.

Historic Forts in Nizwa: Nizwa is a medieval city with several well-preserved forts, notably

Nizwa Fort and Jabreen Castle. These forts provide an insight into Oman's rich cultural past while also serving as interesting sites for corporate events.

Rooftop Lounges in Muscat: The Chedi Muscat's rooftop lounge, which overlooks the city skyline, is an attractive setting for business meetings. It is a popular choice for social and professional events because of its wonderful environment and stunning views.

Yacht Clubs in Muscat and Salalah: High-end yacht clubs such as the Salalah Marina Yacht Club and the Royal Oman Yacht Club are located in Oman's busy ports. These clubs provide classy settings for social events and business gatherings on private yachts.

Private Villas in Muscat: High-end gathering places and executive getaways can be found in opulent private villas like the Royal Estates at Barr Al Jissah in Muscat. These villas' calm atmosphere and individualized services make them an unforgettable venue for business gatherings.

CHAPTER NINE

Resources

Emergency Contacts

in any destination, it's important for travelers to be prepared for any emergencies that may arise during their visit. Knowing the appropriate contacts for emergencies can provide peace of mind and ensure swift assistance when needed. Here are some essential emergency contacts for travelers in Oman:

Police: In case of emergencies requiring police assistance, travelers can dial 999 for immediate help. The Royal Oman Police (ROP) is responsible for maintaining law and order throughout the country and responding to various emergencies, including accidents, theft, and other criminal incidents.

Ambulance: For medical emergencies requiring urgent medical attention or transportation to the hospital, travelers can dial 999 to request an ambulance. The emergency medical services provided by the Ministry of Health are equipped to handle a wide range of medical emergencies, including accidents, injuries, and illnesses.

Fire Department: In the event of a fire or other emergencies requiring firefighting assistance, travelers can dial 999 to contact the fire department. Trained firefighters are available to respond to fires, rescue operations, and other emergencies involving hazardous materials or structural damage.

Coast Guard: For emergencies at sea or along the coast, such as boating accidents, drowning incidents, or maritime distress calls, travelers can contact the Oman Coast Guard by dialing 999. The Coast Guard is responsible for maritime search and rescue operations, as well as maritime law enforcement and safety.

Embassy or Consulate: Travelers should also have the contact information for their respective embassy or consulate in Oman in case of emergencies involving passport loss, legal issues, or other consular services. The embassy or consulate can provide assistance and support to travelers from their home country.

Oman Tourism Police: The Tourism Police in Oman are dedicated to ensuring the safety and security of tourists visiting the country. Travelers can seek assistance from the Tourism Police for issues related to tourism, such as lost or stolen belongings, scams, or harassment. The Tourism Police can be reached by dialing 800 7 9999.

Ministry of Health Hotline: The Ministry of Health in Oman operates a hotline for general inquiries and information related to health services, medical facilities, and public health measures. Travelers can contact the Ministry of Health hotline at 2444 1199 for non-emergency medical assistance and advice.

Road Assistance: In case of car breakdowns or accidents on the road, travelers can contact the Oman Automobile Association (OAA) for roadside assistance and towing services. The OAA operates a 24-hour helpline at 800 7 3000 for roadside assistance and emergency vehicle recovery.

By being aware of these essential emergency contacts and keeping them handy during their travels, travelers can ensure their safety and well-being while exploring the diverse landscapes and cultural treasures of Oman.

Useful Apps

Useful Apps for Traveling in Oman

In today's digital age, travelers to Oman can enhance their journey by utilizing a range of useful apps designed to provide valuable assistance and enhance their overall experience. From navigation aids to language translation tools, these apps offer convenience, accessibility, and essential information at your fingertips.

Google Maps: For travelers seeking seamless navigation throughout Oman's diverse landscapes and cities, Google Maps stands as a reliable ally. This comprehensive mapping app offers detailed directions, real-time traffic updates, and points of interest, ensuring efficient and stress-free travel from one destination to another. Additionally, Google Maps enables users to explore offline maps, making it particularly useful in areas with limited internet connectivity.

Google Translate: In the realm of language translation, Google Translate emerges as an invaluable tool for bridging communication barriers in Oman. With support for multiple languages, including Arabic, users can easily translate text, speech, and even images in real-time. Whether interacting with locals, deciphering signs, or navigating menus, Google Translate facilitates smoother communication and fosters meaningful connections with Oman's people and culture.

Instagram: For travelers seeking to capture and document their experiences in Oman, the Instagram app offers a platform for sharing moments and memories with friends, family, and fellow travelers. With its user-friendly interface and array of creative tools, Instagram allows users to showcase the beauty of Oman's landscapes, architecture, and cultural traditions through captivating photos and videos. Additionally, the platform serves as a source of inspiration, enabling travelers to discover hidden gems and insider tips shared by other users.

Booking.com: When looking of accommodation, the Booking.com app emerges as a valuable resource for finding and booking hotels, guesthouses, and vacation rentals in Oman. With its extensive database of properties, detailed descriptions, and user reviews, Booking.com offers travelers a comprehensive selection of accommodation options tailored to their preferences and budget. Additionally, the app provides secure booking capabilities, flexible cancellation policies, and 24/7 customer support, ensuring peace of mind throughout the booking process.

Zomato: For travelers seeking to explore Oman's culinary scene, the Zomato app offers a wealth of information on restaurants, cafes, and eateries across the country. With its extensive database of dining establishments, user reviews, and ratings, Zomato helps travelers discover hidden culinary gems, sample local delicacies, and plan memorable dining experiences. Additionally, the app provides essential information such as menu details, opening hours, and contact information, making it easy for travelers to find the perfect dining spot wherever they may be.

Travel Insurance

Travel insurance is crucial for travelers as it provides financial protection against unforeseen events such as medical emergencies, trip cancellations, and lost luggage. Securing travel insurance for your journey to Oman is a straightforward process that can be completed through various channels. Here's a detailed guide on how to obtain travel insurance:

1. **Research Insurance Providers:** Start by researching reputable insurance providers that offer comprehensive travel insurance coverage. Look for companies with a strong track record, positive customer reviews, and policies tailored to your specific needs.

2. **Compare Policies:** Once you've identified potential insurance providers, compare their policies to determine which offers the best coverage for your trip to

Oman. Consider factors such as coverage limits, exclusions, deductibles, and additional benefits.

3. **Choose the Right Coverage:** Select a travel insurance policy that aligns with your travel plans and provides adequate coverage for potential risks. Consider factors such as the duration of your trip, the activities you'll be engaging in, and any pre-existing medical conditions that may require special coverage.

4. **Review Policy Details:** Before purchasing a travel insurance policy, carefully review the terms and conditions, coverage limits, and exclusions outlined in the policy documents. Pay close attention to any pre-existing medical conditions that may affect coverage eligibility and inquire about any additional riders or add-ons available for enhanced protection.

5. **Obtain a Quote:** Once you've chosen a travel insurance policy that meets your needs, obtain a quote from the insurance provider. The quote will outline the cost of the policy based on factors such as trip duration, coverage limits, and any optional add-ons selected.

6. **Purchase the Policy:** After reviewing the quote and ensuring that the policy meets your requirements, proceed to purchase the travel insurance policy. You can typically purchase insurance online through the provider's website or by contacting their customer service team directly.

7. **Provide Travel Details:** When purchasing the travel insurance policy, you'll need to provide details about your trip to Oman, including travel dates, destinations, and any planned activities. This information will help the insurance

provider tailor the policy to your specific travel itinerary.

8. **Make Payment:** Complete the purchase of the travel insurance policy by making the required payment through the provider's preferred payment method. Be sure to review the payment details carefully to ensure accuracy and confirm that the policy is successfully activated.

9. **Receive Policy Documents:** After purchasing the travel insurance policy, you'll receive confirmation of coverage along with policy documents outlining the terms and conditions of the insurance policy. Keep these documents handy during your travels to Oman for reference in case of emergencies.

10. **Contact Customer Service:** If you have any questions or need assistance during the purchasing process, don't hesitate to contact the insurance provider's customer

service team for guidance. They can provide clarification on policy details, assist with completing the purchase, and address any concerns you may have.

By following these steps, you can easily obtain travel insurance coverage for your journey to Oman.

Common Phrases

Being familiar with common phrases in Arabic can greatly enhance travelers' experiences and facilitate communication with locals. While English is widely spoken, particularly in urban areas and tourist destinations, demonstrating an effort to speak Arabic is appreciated and often leads to warmer interactions. Here are some essential phrases to help travelers navigate their way through Oman with ease:

- **Greetings and Pleasantries**

"As-salamu alaykum" (Peace be upon you) - This is the traditional Arabic greeting, to which the response is "Wa alaykum as-salam" (And peace be upon you).

"Marhaban" (Welcome) - A friendly way to greet someone or express hospitality.

"Sabah al-khayr" (Good morning) - Used to greet someone in the morning.

"Masa' al-khayr" (Good evening) - Used to greet someone in the evening.

"Shukran" (Thank you) - An expression of gratitude.

- **Basic Communication**

"Min fadlak" (Please) - Used when making a request or asking for something politely.

"Afwan" (You're welcome) - A response to "Shukran" (Thank you).

"Kayfa halak?" (How are you?) - A common way to inquire about someone's well-being.
"Ana bikhair, shukran" (I'm fine, thank you) - A typical response to "Kayfa halak?"

- **Navigating and Directions**

"Wayn al-hammaam?" (Where is the bathroom?) - Useful when asking for directions to the restroom.

"Kaifa yasiru ila..." (How do I get to...) - Helpful for asking directions to a specific location.

"Al-jihaad huna" (It's this way) - A response to someone asking for directions.
Shopping and Dining:

"Bi-kam hatha?" (How much is this?) - Useful when inquiring about the price of an item.

"Hal yujad huna mahal li'akal?" (Is there a restaurant nearby?) - Helpful when looking for a place to eat.

"Ana ureedu..." (I would like...) - Used when ordering food or making a purchase.

- **Emergencies**

"Al-Musaa'ada!" (Help!) - Used in emergency situations when assistance is needed.

"Hada wadha'un" (This is an emergency) - A phrase to emphasize the urgency of the situation. Miscellaneous:

"Ayna tajidu al-taksi?" (Where can I find a taxi?) - Useful when looking for transportation.

"Hatha jayidun" (This is good) - Used to express satisfaction or approval.

"La afham" *(I don't understand)* - Helpful when encountering language barriers.
Expressing Politeness:

"Al-'afw" (Excuse me) - Used to get someone's attention or when passing through a crowded area.

"Tafadhil" (Please) - Another way to politely make a request or gesture for someone to go ahead of you.

- **Making Small Talk**

"Ma ismuk?" *(What is your name?)* - A friendly way to initiate conversation and learn someone's name.

"Min ayna 'anta?" *(Where are you from?)* - A common question when meeting someone new.

- **Expressing Appreciation**

"Jameel" (Beautiful) - Used to compliment something or express admiration.
"Mumtaz" (Excellent) - Another way to convey praise or approval.

- **Seeking Assistance**

"Hal tasta'mil haatif?" (Do you speak English?) - Helpful for determining if someone can communicate in English.

"Hal tatakallam al-lugha al-'arabiyya?" (Do you speak Arabic?) - Useful for communicating in the local language.

- **Time and Dates**

"Saa'a kam?" (What time is it?) - Useful for checking the time.

"Yawm al-jum'ah" (Friday) - The holiest day of the week in Islam, when many businesses may have adjusted hours.

- **Expressing Concern**

"Hal anta bikhair?" (Are you okay?) - A caring inquiry to check on someone's well-being.

"Ma hadha?" (What is this?) - Used when encountering something unfamiliar or unexpected.

- **Traveling Logistics**

"Hal hunaka makan li al-talab?" (Is there a place to charge?) - Useful when needing to charge electronic devices.

"Hal tatawajaf al-Internet hunaa?" (Is there Wi-Fi here?) - Important for staying connected while traveling.

- **Social Interactions**

"Hal yujad huna 'aynaat sharaab?" (Are there any drinking fountains here?) - Helpful when looking for water sources in public spaces.

"Ayna tajidu al-ta'amil?" (Where can you find food?) - Useful for finding restaurants or food stalls.

- **Farewells**

"Ma'a as-salama" (Goodbye) - A formal way to bid farewell.

"Allah ma'ak" (God be with you) - Another way to say goodbye, often used in a more heartfelt manner.

Travelers can enhance their experience in Oman by familiarizing themselves with common phrases that are used in the region. Even though English may be sufficient in many cases, attempting to speak Arabic will not only demonstrate respect for the local culture and customs but also show appreciation for Oman's heritage. This will help to build deeper connections with the people and enrich your overall experience.

Language Etiquette

Travelers can enhance their experience and build rapport with locals by adhering to certain language etiquette norms

Learn Basic Arabic Phrases: While English is commonly understood, making an effort to learn basic Arabic phrases can greatly enrich your interactions with locals. Greetings such as "As-salamu alaykum" (Peace be upon you) and "Marhaban" (Welcome) are appreciated gestures that convey respect and appreciation for the local culture.

Use Formal Language: When addressing others, particularly elders or individuals in positions of authority, it is important to use formal language and titles. For example, addressing someone as "Sayyid" (Sir) or "Sayyida" (Madam) followed by their last name demonstrates politeness and respect.

Be Mindful of Cultural Sensitivities: Oman is a conservative society, and certain topics may be considered taboo or sensitive. Avoid discussing politics, religion, or personal matters unless invited to do so by your host. Additionally, be mindful of modesty in dress and behavior, particularly in rural or traditional areas.

Practice Active Listening: Demonstrating active listening skills, such as maintaining eye contact, nodding, and avoiding interruptions, shows respect and attentiveness to the speaker. Avoid multitasking or checking your phone during conversations, as this can be perceived as rude or disrespectful.

Seek Permission Before Taking Photos: When photographing individuals, particularly women or religious sites, always seek permission first. Respect the privacy and cultural sensitivities of others, and refrain from taking photos in restricted areas or during prayer times.

Be Patient and Courteous: Patience and courtesy are valued virtues in Omani culture. If faced with language barriers or misunderstandings, remain patient and avoid displaying frustration. Use gestures, simple language, or translation apps to facilitate communication, and always express gratitude for any assistance received.

Avoid Using Slang or Colloquialisms: While slang or colloquial expressions may be common in casual conversations, it is best to avoid using them when interacting with strangers or in formal settings. Stick to standard language and expressions to ensure clarity and mutual understanding.

Express Gratitude: Expressing gratitude is an important aspect of language etiquette in Oman. Use phrases such as "Shukran" (Thank you) and "Afwan" (You're welcome) to show appreciation for acts of kindness or assistance.

Conclusion and Additional Tips

Safety Tips

- Plan your route and familiarize yourself with the area before exploring.
- Keep a charged mobile phone with you for communication.
- Dress appropriately, especially in conservative areas, to avoid unwanted attention.
- Avoid wandering off alone in unfamiliar or remote areas.
- Be cautious when engaging in outdoor activities like hiking and swimming.
- Check weather forecasts and avoid traveling during severe weather conditions.
- Secure your accommodation and vehicles properly.

- Avoid sharing personal details or sensitive information with strangers.
- Learn basic Arabic phrases for communication in emergencies.
- Stay informed about local laws and regulations to avoid unintentional violations.
- Be respectful and patient in interactions with locals and avoid confrontations.
- Keep emergency contact information and insurance details accessible.
- Trust your instincts and avoid situations or places that feel unsafe.
- Be mindful of belongings and avoid displaying valuables in public.
- Stay aware of surroundings, especially in crowded areas.
- Use caution when crossing streets and be mindful of traffic.
- Respect local customs and traditions, especially when visiting religious sites.
- Avoid public displays of affection.

- Observe speed limits and drive cautiously, especially on mountainous and desert roads.
- Ensure that seatbelts are worn by all passengers while driving.
- Be aware of road conditions, especially during inclement weather.
- Check rental car safety features before driving.
- Familiarize yourself with Oman's driving regulations, including speed limits and traffic laws.
- Stay hydrated by drinking plenty of water, especially in Oman's hot and dry climate.
- Use sunscreen, wear protective clothing, and seek shade to avoid sunburn and heatstroke.
- Be cautious when consuming food and water, especially in rural areas.
- Use insect repellent to prevent mosquito bites and protect against mosquito-borne diseases.
- Seek medical attention promptly if you experience any health issues.

- Know emergency contact numbers, including local authorities and embassy information.
- Carry copies of important documents such as passports, visas, and travel insurance information.
- Stay informed about any health advisories or travel alerts related to Oman.

Sustainable Travel Tips

To ensure the suitability of the text for a business or academic setting, it is crucial to adhere to formal language conventions, avoid contractions, and maintain clarity, conciseness, and accuracy throughout the content.

Sustainable travel encompasses practices that minimize negative impacts on the environment, support local communities, and contribute to the preservation of cultural heritage. For travelers visiting Oman, adopting sustainable travel tips not only benefits the destination but also enhances the overall travel experience.

One essential sustainable travel tip is to reduce carbon emissions by opting for eco-friendly transportation options whenever possible. This may include using public transportation, cycling, or walking to explore destinations, thus minimizing reliance on fossil fuel-powered vehicles and reducing air pollution.

Conserving water and energy is another key aspect of sustainable travel. Travelers can contribute to water conservation efforts by taking shorter showers, reusing towels and linens, and being mindful of water usage when brushing teeth or doing dishes. Similarly, conserving energy can be achieved by turning off lights, air conditioning, and electronic devices when not in use, as well as choosing accommodations that prioritize energy efficiency.

Supporting local businesses and cultural heritage is integral to sustainable travel practices. Travelers can patronize locally owned hotels, restaurants, and shops, thereby stimulating the local economy and preserving traditional craftsmanship and culinary traditions. Additionally, participating in cultural activities and visiting heritage sites allows travelers to gain a deeper appreciation for Oman's rich cultural heritage while supporting efforts to safeguard it for future generations.

Engaging in responsible wildlife tourism is another important consideration for sustainable travel in Oman. Travelers should avoid activities that exploit or harm wildlife, such as riding captive animals or purchasing products made from endangered species. Instead, they can support conservation initiatives and eco-friendly wildlife experiences that prioritize animal welfare and environmental sustainability.

Emphasizing the natural beauty and cultural diversity of Oman reinforces the importance of protecting these assets through sustainable travel practices. By following practical advice that promotes sustainability without compromising comfort or enjoyment, travelers can contribute to the preservation of Oman's environment, support local communities, and create meaningful travel experiences for themselves and future generations.

Final Recommendations

Hey there! As you get ready to embark on your journey through Oman, we've got some recommendations to share with you that can make your experience even more amazing. We want you to have the best time possible, so we hope you find these tips helpful.

First and foremost, it's super important to respect local customs, traditions, and cultural sensitivities during your travels in Oman. The Omani people are known for their hospitality and warmth, so by being courteous and considerate towards locals, you can make some great connections and learn so much about the local culture.

Next up, we encourage you to practice responsible and sustainable travel habits, which is crucial in preserving Oman's natural beauty for future generations. This includes things like reducing waste, conserving water and energy, and supporting eco-friendly initiatives wherever you can. By being mindful of your impact on the environment, you can help keep Oman's stunning landscapes and biodiversity in great shape.

Now, Oman has so much to offer when it comes to adventure and exploration. From ancient forts and bustling souks to rugged mountains and pristine waters, there's something for everyone. Be open to new experiences, engage with local communities, and let yourself be captivated by the beauty and charm of this amazing destination.

Of course, we want you to stay safe during your travels in Oman too. When you're exploring remote areas or engaging in outdoor activities, exercise caution and use common sense. Be prepared for changes in weather conditions, stay hydrated, and always follow any safety warnings or advice from local authorities. By taking care of yourself, you can enjoy your travels in Oman with peace of mind.

Finally, don't forget to indulge in the delicious flavors of Omani cuisine. From aromatic spices and succulent meats to fresh seafood and sweet treats, Oman offers a culinary journey that is sure to delight your taste buds. Make sure you try local specialties like shuwa (slow-cooked lamb), harees (wheat and meat porridge), and halwa (a sweet dessert made from sugar, ghee, and rosewater) for a truly authentic culinary experience.

We hope you find these recommendations helpful and that they help you get the most out of your trip to Oman. By keeping the principles of respect, sustainability, adventure, and culinary exploration in mind, we're sure you'll have a fantastic time full of wonderful memories. Whether you're an experienced traveler or a first-time visitor, we wish you a journey filled with joy, discovery, and lots of fun!

Printed in Great Britain
by Amazon